MUCH
MUFFINS

Louise Pepper

authorHOUSE®

AuthorHouse™
1663 Liberty Drive
Bloomington, IN 47403
www.authorhouse.com
Phone: 1-800-839-8640

Published by AuthorHouse 3/1/2012

ISBN: 978-1-4685-5271-3 (sc)
ISBN 978-1-4685-5270-6 (e)

Library of Congress Control Number: 2012903004

When I first began my writing development process it was for the purpose of creating novels, however people, even writers need nutrition, so on my ventures into the kitchen I began to keep track of what was happening there.

Having completed **Borscht & Beyond**, on to **Book of Beans**, followed by **Much Muffins**. Intersected only briefly by **Got Your Back,** a children's novel of caring and sharing. Then perhaps finally, to that long awaited novel.

Much Muffins was originally to be titled *Have you seen this Muffin Ma'am?* Cute, but did not make the cut. So while I go back to the creation of that Great Romantic novel…..

Do have a Muffin! Bon Appetite!

Who does not love muffins? We bake them, we buy them, we give and are given them as offerings of friendship, kindness, peace, reward or just a plain response to hunger.

The word muffin is derived from the French word *moufflet*, which is often applied to breads and means soft. Two main muffins are English muffins and American style sweet muffins. They vary in style as well as flavor and history.

Muffins became widely used as a breakfast food because they were easy to prepare and cook in a short period of time. Because muffins grew stale so quickly, they were not marketed as a baked good until the middle of the 20th century. Recipes were limited to certain types of grains and simple additives like nuts and dried fruits. When paper muffin cups were invented, non-stick pans have allowed muffins to be baked with a variety of fun ingredients, however, circular muffins remain the most popular. Packaged muffins mixes were introduced to the market place in the 1950's. Muffins were marketed as an alternative to donuts in the 1960's.

English muffins are a flat yeast raised muffin with nooks and crannies cooked on a hot griddle. Their history dates back to the 10th and 11th Centuries.

American style muffins are more of a quick bread that is made in individual molds sometime decorated as mini cakes.

Muffin recipes first appeared in print in the mid 18th century and quickly caught on. By the 19th century Muffin Men walked the streets of England at tea time selling muffins.

Apple Cheese Muffins

½ cup vegetable shortening

½ cup sugar

1½ cup all purpose flour

2 eggs

1 tsp. baking powder

1 tsp baking soda

¾ cup quick cooking rolled oats

½ tsp salt

1 cup finely chopped apples

½ cup chopped pecans

¾ cup milk

¼ cup butter

12 thin slices unpeeled cored red apples

⅔ cup coarsely grated sharp cheddar cheese

¼ cup cinnamon mixed with 3 Tbsp. sugar

Cream shortening and sugar, add eggs one at a time beating well after each addition. Mix and sift flour, baking powder, baking soda, and salt; Stir into creamed mixture. Sir in oats, chopped apples, cheese and pecans; mix well. Add milk gradually stir to just moisten other ingredients.

Fill well-greased muffin cups two–thirds full each. Dip apple slices into melted butter, then in cinnamon sugar. Press one slice into batter of each muffin cup. Sprinkle slightly with cinnamon sugar. Bake in reheated 400 degree oven for 25 minutes.

Filling:

8 oz. softened cream cheese	⅓ cup sugar
2 Tbsp all purpose flour	1 tsp. vanilla

Batter:

2-½ cups all purpose flour	2 cups sugar
2 ½ tsp baking soda	1 tsp salt
1 Tbsp cinnamon	½ tsp nutmeg
3 – ½ cups raisin bran cereal	2 large eggs lightly beaten
2 cups well shaken buttermilk	½ cup vegetable oil
½ cup raisins or nuts	

Preheat oven to 400 degrees spray 24 muffin cup pans or line with paper liner.

Make Filling: Stir filling ingredients until well combined. Keep filling covered and chilled.

Make Batter: Sift together flour, sugar, baking soda, salt, cinnamon, and nutmeg, stir in cereal. Add eggs, buttermilk, oil and raisins, stirring until well combined. Batter may be kept chilled & covered till ready to bake (about 1 week)

Spoon heaping tablespoon of batter into each cup top with 2 tablespoons of filling. Spoon 1 heaping tablespoon batter over the filling, spread to cover filling completely.

Bake muffins mid oven for 20 – 25 minutes.

Amazing Rye & Oatmeal Muffins

1 cup rye flour

1 Tsp baking powder

4 eggs

2 Tsp vanilla

¼ cup chopped dried apricots

1 ¼ sticks softened butter or melted margarine

1 cup quick cooking oats

1 Tsp salt

1 cup brown sugar

1 cup chopped walnuts

Mix first 4 ingredients together, set aside.

Beat eggs, sugar vanilla and butter (margarine) together

Just till dry ingredients are moistened.

Fill oiled or paper cup lined muffin tins and bake in a pre-heated oven at 350 degrees for 30 – 40 minutes till brown . Test centre with toothpick for doneness. If nothing sticks they are done if it sticks muffins need a few more minutes of baking, keep checking for Doneness.

Make 12 – 15 muffins.

Best Ever Bran Muffins

1 – 15 oz. package Raisin Bran cereal

5 cups flour

5 tsp. baking soda

1 ½ cup chopped walnuts

1 cup vegetable shortening

3 cups sugar

1 Tsp salt

4 beaten eggs

1 quart buttermilk, well shaken.

Sift first six dry ingredients together over layer of wax paper.

Cream together eggs and vegetable shortening and buttermilk.

Pick up wax paper folding slightly to form trough and add dry ingredients to creamed mixture and mix well. Place into a covered container and may be stored up to 6 weeks.

Fill oil sprayed or paper lined muffin cups up to ⅔ full.

Bake at 400 degrees for approximately 15 minutes.

Brown Sugar Pecan Muffins

1 cup brown sugar	½ cup softened butter or margarine
1 egg	1 cup milk
½ Tsp salt	½ Tsp baking soda
1 Tsp baking powder	2 cups flour
½ cup chopped pecans	½ Tsp vanilla

Cream butter (margarine) with sugar in a medium bowl. Add egg (slightly beaten) and milk, stir well to combine. Mix together dry ingredients add to sugar mixture. Stir in nuts and vanilla. Fill greased muffin pans ⅔ full bake at 400 degrees for 12 – 15 minutes.

Cappuccino Muffins

2 cups all purpose flour	½ cup sugar
2-½ Tsp baking powder	2 Tsp instant coffee powder
½ Tsp salt	½ Tsp cinnamon
1 cup scalded and cool milk	½ cup melted and cooled butter
1 egg slightly beaten	1 Tsp vanilla extract
¾ cup semi-sweet chocolate mini-chips	

Grease or line with paper 12 or 24 muffin cups.

Stir moist ingredients until blended

Comine dry ingredients until well blended,

Fold in moist ingredients till blended

Stir in Chocolate Chips

Spoon I nto muffin tins

Bake 15 – 20 minutes at 375 degrees .

After cooling May be frozen for future use.

Make 12 regular and 24 mini muffins.

Crunchy Cranberry Buttermilk Muffins

1 ⅓ cups all purpose flour

⅔ cup instant cooking rolled oats, uncooked

1 ½ Tsp baking powder   ⅓ cup firm packed brown sugar

1 Tsp baking soda   ½ Tsp cinnamon

½ Tsp nutmeg   ¼ Tsp salt

¾ cup buttermilk   1 egg slightly beaten

¼ cup melted butter   ½ chopped fresh or dried cranberries

Preheat oven to 400 degrees F. Combine dry ingredients in a large mixing bowl. Combine liquid ingredients in a smaller mixing bowl. Stir liquid mixture into dry mixture just until dry ingredients are moistened.

Gently stir in cranberries. Fill paper lined muffin pans to ⅔ full. Bake for 20 – 25 minutes or until wooden pickl inserted in centre comes out clean. Cool on wire rack for 10 minutes. Serve with warm or cold butter.

Muffins may be made ahead and frozen, Reheat for 30 – 45 seconds.

Dilly Zucchini Muffins

1 ½ cups flour   2 Tbsp sugar

3 Tsp baking powder   ½ Tsp salt

¾ Tsp dill weed   ¼ cup milk

½ cup melted margarine   2 eggs

⅔ cup ricotta cheese   ½ cup grated zucchini

Preheat oven to 400 degrees F.

Combine flour, sugar, baking powder, salt and dill weed, in a large bowl , mix well.

Combine milk, melted margarine and eggs in a medium bowl.
Stir in ricotta cheese and zucchini, beat well. Add to dry ingredients Stirring just to moisten. Batter will be stiff.

Fill 12 muffin tins lined with muffin paper or sprayed with non-stick oil to ⅔ full. Bake 20-25 minutes till golden brown.

Fresh Ginger Muffins

1 – 2 ounce piece of unpeeled ginger root

2 cups flour	¾ cup plus 3 Tbsp sugar
½ Tsp salt	2 Tbsp lemon zest from 2 lemons
¾ Tsp baking soda	½ cup butter at room temperature
2 eggs	1 cup butter milk

Preheat oven to 375 degrees Grease muffin tins or line with muffin paper. Cut unpeeled ginger into large hunks. If you have a food processor process ginger into tiny pieces or chop by hand. You should have about ¼ cup . It is better to have too much ginger than too little. Put ginger and ¼ cup sugar into a small skillet and cook over medium heat until sugar is melted and mixture is hot. . Do not leave pot unattended on stove. Remove from stove and let ginger mixture cool. Put lemon zest and 3 Tbsp sugar into food processor and process until lemon peel is well chopped, Add to ginger mixture. Stir and set aside. Put butter in a mixing bowl. Beat and add remaining ½ cup sugar, beat until smooth. Add eggs and beat well. Add buttermilk and mix until blended. Add remaining dry ingredients and beat until smooth. Mix in ginger lemon mixture. Spoon batter inot muffin tins so that each cup is ⅔ full. Bake 15 – 20 minutes. Serve warm.

Gold Ribbon Fibre Muffins

1 cup margarine

1 cup sugar

2 eggs

1 – ½ cups whole wheat flour

½ cup regular flour

2 ½ Tsp baking soda

2 cups buttermilk

1 cup 100% bran

1 cup boiling water

2 cups All Bran

½ Tsp salt

1 cup ground walnuts

1 cup raisins

½ cup wheat germ.

Cream margarine and sugar. Add eggs and beat. Sift flours with baking soda. Add creamed mixture alternating with buttermilk. Mix well. Combine 100% bran with water, add to batter and stir in. Fold in All Bran salt walnuts raisins and wheat germ.

You can keep batter in the refrigerator for up to two weeks in a wide mouth jar, bake as needed. Bake at 400 degrees for 15 – 20 minutes.

Fruit Muffins

6 Tbsp butter

2 eggs

¾ cup milk

½ Tsp salt

½ cup raisins

½ cup chopped walnuts

1- ¼ cups sugar

1 cup All-bran cereal

2 cups flour

2 Tsp baking powder

½ cup chopped dates

Cream butter and sugar together. Add slightly beaten eggs and blend well. Add bran and milk. Let sit a few minute so bran softens.

Add flour salt and baking powder. Mix well. Add dates, raisins and nuts. For added flavour add dried cranberries and/or dried cherries.

Bake at 375 degrees for 25 minutes.

Ginger Sweet Potato Muffins

1 – ¾ cups all purpose flour

¾ cup firmly packed brown sugar

¾ cup mashed baked sweet potato, cooled

2 Tsp baking powder   ¼ Tsp baking soda

¼ Tsp salt   ½ Tsp ground cinnamon

¼ Tsp ground ginger   ½ cup fat free milk

2 large eggs lightly beaten   3 Tbsp canola oil

1 – ½ tsp vanilla extract

¼ to ⅓ cup finely chopped crystallized ginger.

Preheat oven 375 degrees. Lightly coat 12 muffin tins with non-stick oil or line with paper cups.

In a large bowl, stir together flour, brown sugar, baking powder, salt, cinnamon and ground ginger. In another bowl, stir together sweet potato, milk, eggs oil and vanilla, until blended. Make a well in the centre of the dry ingredients add milk mixture and stir just to combine. Stir in ginger.

Spoon batter into prepared muffin tins. Bake 15 – 20 minutes,

Remove muffins from oven, cool 5 minutes before removing To finish cooling. Serve warm or completely cooled, store in an airtight container at room temperature.

Harvey Wallbanger Muffins

1 box yellow cake mix, (not jiffy mix)

1 cup grape seed oil

¼ cup Galliano Liqueur

1- 3 oz. pkg. Vanilla instant pudding mix

4 eggs

¼ cup vodka

¾ cup orange juice

Glaze... follows

Preheat oven to 350 degrees, Mix all ingredients for 3 minutes at medium speed on hand mixer.

Glaze:

1 cup sifted icing sugar

1 Tbsp Galliano

1 Tbsp orange juice

1 Tsp Vodka

Mix all together , pour over warm muffins.

Fill mini-muffin or regular paper lined muffin tins ¾ full. Bake fro 10 minutes if mini muffins or 20 minutes if regular sized pans. Check for doneness with toothpick inserted in centre.
If it comes out clean... they are done!!!!!

Honey Bran Muffins

1- ¼ cup grape seed oil

4 egg whites and 1 whole egg

½ cup unbleached white flour

1 Tbsp baking soda

¾ cup warm water

2 cups buttermilk

¾ cup honey

2-cups whole wheat flour

½ cup wheat germ

1 Tsp salt

4 cups bran flakes

Cream oil, honey. Add 1 egg at a time and beat until blended. Stir in flour, soda and salt. Add wheat germ. Add to the creamed mixture, alternately with warm water. Stir in bran flakes and buttermilk.

When ready to bake, spoon into greased muffin tins to ⅔ full and bake at 375 degrees for 20 minutes. Whole recipe makes about 20 medium sized muffins.

If you prefer sweet muffins, add all or part of the following combinations : Raisins and grated lemon rind, chopped dates and grated orange rind, frozen blueberries, chopped nuts, chopped apples chopped banana and any other handy fruit.

Batter will keep in refrigerator for a week up to 10 days.

Huckleberry Muffins

1 cup huckleberries

2 cups all purpose flour

½ tsp salt

4 Tbsp melted margerine

¼ cup milk

½ cup brown sugar

1 Tbsp baking powder

2 eggs

1 Tsp vanilla

¼ cup corn syrup

Combine sugar and huckleberries. Stir in flour, baking powder and salt. In a separate bowl beat together eggs, milk vanilla margarine and syrup. Combine the two mixtures using a fork. Do not over mix.

Fill paper lined muffin tins , ¾ full. Bake at 450 degrees for 20 – 25 minutes.

Ice Box Muffin Mix

2 cups boiling water

1 cup Vegetable Shortening

4 beaten eggs

5 cups flour

4 cups All Bran or Bran Bud Cereal

2 cups 100 % Bran Cereal

3 cups sugar

1 quart buttermilk

5 Tsp baking soda

1 Tbsp salt

Mix water, 100% bran, shortening, sugar, eggs, buttermilk in a large bowl

In a separate bowl mix dry ingredients: flour, salt and soda.

Mix the two mixtures together. Lastly add All bran or Bran buds. Now ready for use or cover tightly in a container and refrigerate. It will keep this way for 2 months. When you wish to use, spoon into paper lined muffins tins to ¾ full. You may add chopped dates or raisins.

Bake at 400 degrees for 15 minutes.

Kona Coffee Cup Muffins

¼ cup melted margarine   ½ cup sugar

2 eggs   2 cups flour

2 ½ Tsp baking powder   ½ cup milk

¼ cup strong coffee (Kona Coffee best)

Blend margarine, sugar, and eggs until creamy. Add sifted flour and baking powder. Add milk.

Spray 9 heat proof coffee cups with non-stick oil

Fill half full with batter.

Drop 1 Tsp of jam n the centre of each and add more batter to each cup.

Place cups on a cookie sheet

Bake at 350 degree oven for 30 minutes.

Serve cups on saucers.

Light as Air Oatmeal Muffins

1 cup dry oatmeal

1 cup flour

1- ½ Tsp baking powder

1 egg

¼ cup melted butter

1 cup buttermilk

½ Tsp salt

½ Tsp baking soda

½ cup dark brown sugar

Preheat oven to 400 degrees and prepare muffin tins.

Place oatmeal in a bowl. Pour buttermilk over it.

Let stand while sifting together, flour, salt, baking powder, and baking soda.

Beat the egg into the oatmeal mixture, then beat in the brown sugar. Stir in the sifted dry ingredients and then the melted butter.

So not over mix.

Pour batter to ⅔ filled into greased muffin tins and bake about 18 minutes.

Low Sugar Oatmeal Muffins

1 cup uncooked, quick cooking oats

1 pkg. pre mixed plain muffin mix (12 muffin size)

1 egg. Beaten well with a slotted spoon or whisk

1 cup buttermilk   ½ Tsp baking soda

¼ cup brown sugar, packed well   ⅓ cup grape seed oil

Combine oats and buttermilk. Let soak while you do the rest.

Spray a muffin pan with non-stik spray.

Set oven to 400 degrees.

Mix together, muffin mix, baking soda and brown sugar.

Stir well.

Add oats and milk mixture, egg and oil. Mix well.

Spoon into muffin pans. Bake 20 – 25 minutes until brown

Maple-Apricot Oatmeal Muffins

2 cups rolled oats

⅔ dark maple syrup

2 eggs, beaten

2 Tsp baking powder

2 Tsp salt

½ cup dried apricots, chopped

2 cups buttermilk

⅔ cup vegetable shortening

2 cups white floour

1 Tsp baking soda

1/8 cup brown sugar

Combine oats, buttermilk, maple syrup and apricots, soak over night.

Next day stir in shortening, eggs. Combine flour, baking powder, baking soda, salt ,brown sugar Gradually fold Maplesyrup mixture into the batter.

Drop batter by spoon fulls into buttered or paper lined muffins cups, to ⅔ full

Sprinkle tops with brown sugar and bake at 400 degrees for 20 - 25 minutes.

Mighty Muffins

1 – ½ cups whole bran cereal
2 slightly beaten egg whites
¼ cup grape seed oil
½ cup whole wheat flour
½ Tsp baking soda
½ cup raisins or any other dried fruit you prefer.

1 cup skim milk
⅓ cup molasses
½ cup all purpose flour
2 Tbsp wheat germ
2 Tsp baking powder

Mix cereal, milk, and egg whites together and soak 3 minutes. Stir molasses and oil into the bran mixture.

Stir flours, wheat germ, baking soda and baking powder together. Make a well in the centre, add bran mixture and stir to moisten. Fold in fruit. Pour into paper lined muffin tins.

Bake at 400 degrees for 20 – 25 minutes.

Moist Bran Muffins

3 cups sugar

4 large eggs - beaten

2 Tbsp ground cinnamon

2 cans fruit cocktail un drained

1 quart buttermilk

1 cup grape seed oil

2 Tbsp baking soda

2 Tsp salt

5 cups flour

7 ½ cups Raisin bran cereal.

Combine all ingredients in order, in a large mixing bowl, beat at medium speed for 2 minutes. Bake at 400 degrees for 16 – 18 minutes. Batter keeps for up to 2 week refrigerated.

Morning Muffins

2 cups, peeled, cored and finely diced Granny Smith Apples

2 cups carrots, grated   ¾ cup coconut flakes

½ cup raisins   ½ cup slivered almonds

2 cups flour   ¾ cup sugar

1 – ½ Tsp baking soda   ½ Tsp baking powder

1 – ½ Tsp ground cinnamon   ¼ Tsp ground nutmeg

½ Tsp salt   3 eggs

½ cup grape seed oil   ½ cup milk

2 Tsp vanilla

Preheat oven to 375 degrees. Line muffin cups or spray with non stick oil Prepare apples carrots, coconut flakes raisins and almond slivers, toss together, set aside.

Combine dry ingredients and set aside. Beat eggs for 2 minutes, the add oil, milk, and vanilla, mix well. Add dry ingredients Mix until blended. Fold in remaining ingredients.

Bake 375 degrees for 25 – 28 minutes . Do not over bake.

For quick on the go muffins, place batter in lined muffin pans and Freeze. Once frozen, remove muffins from tin and place in a sealable plastic freezer bag until

Ready to use. To bake frozen muffins place muffins in a muffin pan and bake in a preheated 375 degree oven for 30 – 35 minutes. Keep frozen batter for up to 3 weeks.

Northland Bran Muffins

½ cup boiling water	1-½ cups whole bran cereal
1 cup buttermilk	¾ cup sugar
3 eggs	⅓ cup vegetable shortening
2 cups sifted flour	1 ¼ Tsp baking soda
½ Tsp salt	

Pour boiling water over bran cereal. Stir in buttermilk. Cream together sugar and shortening. Add well beaten eggs Stir together flour, baking soda and salt.

Mix bran mixture into creamed sugar and shortening. Add dry ingredients, stir until moist. Can be stored for up to 3 days in a tightly covered container in the Refrigerator.

Fill muffin pans coated with non-stick oil spray or in muffins papers fill to ⅔ full and bake at 350 degrees for approximately 15 – 20 minutes.

Oil Free Muffins

This recipe substitutes corn syrup for oil. Try this with other baking recipes and lower fat content.

2-¼ cups oat bran cereal

¼ brown sugar or maple syrup

2 egg whites

½ cup dry fruits (raisins, blueberries, cranberries dates or prunes)

1 Tbsp baking powder

1 ¼ cup skim milk

2 Tbsp corn syrup

Preheat oven to 425 degrees. Mix dry ingredients in a large bowl. Mix milk, egg whites and corn syrup together and blend with dry ingredients. Line muffin pans with paper baking cups and fill ⅔ full with batter, divided evenly.

Bake 13 – 15 minutes. Test for doneness with a tooth pick inserted in middle of muffin.

Peanut Butter Muffins

3 cups all purpose white flour

1 Tsp salt

¼ cup brown sugar

¼ cup honey

¼ cup peanut butter

1 ¾ cup milk

1 Tbsp baking powder

½ cup dry roasted peanuts

½ cup peanut butter chips

½ cup vegetable oil

3 eggs

2 Tsp vanilla

Topping:

Peanut crumbs

2 Tbsp white sugar.

Chop roasted peanuts into large crumbs by chopping with knife or processing in Food processor, being careful not to over do, peanuts wil become smooth and gooey. Not what you want.

In a medium bowl blend together flour, baking powder, salt, ¼ cup of the peanut crumbs and brown sugar. In a separate bowl stir together remaining ingredients, then pour into flour mixture. Stir till just blended.

Preheat oven to 375 degrees. Fill lined muffin tins to ⅔ full, sprinkle top of each muffin with topping. Bake 25 minutes or until tested baked with toothpick test.

Pecan Orange Muffins

½ cup softened butter or margarine

2 large eggs

1 Tsp baking soda

¾ cup chopped toasted pecans

¼ cup orange juice

1 cup sugar

2 cups all purpose flour

2 cup plain yogurt

1 Tsp grated orange rind

1 Tbsp sugar.

Beat butter at medium speed with electric mixer until creamy. Add eggs one at a time. Beat after each addition to blend well. Combine flour, baking soda add to butter mixture alternate with yogurt, begin and end with flour mixture. Stir in pecans and orange rind.

Line muffin cups with paper baking cups. Spoon batter into cups, to ⅔ full.

Bake at 375 degrees for 18 – 20 minutes, until lightly browned. Remove from oven, brush muffin tops with orange juice and sprinkle with sugar while still warm.

Pennsalvania Pumpkin Muffins

2 – ¼ cups flour	2 Tsp baking powder
½ Tsp baking soda	1 Tsp ground cinnamon
½ Tsp ground nutmeg	½ Tsp salt
1 can canned pumpkin	⅔ cup honey
3/8 cup milk	2 eggs
¼ cup grape seed oli	½ cup chopped walnuts

Preheat oven to 375 degrees. Spray or paper cup line muffin tins.

In a large bowl stir dry ingredients together with a fork. Set aside.

In a smaller bowl combine remaining ingredients except for walnuts. Beat with wooden spoon unitil well blended. Pour into dry ingredients and stir until just blended. Fold in walnuts. Spoon batter into prepared muffins tins.

Bake for 20 -25 minutes. Until done.

Poppy Seed Muffins

3 cups flour

1- ½ Tsp baking powder

¾ cup Grape Seed oil

3 eggs

2- ½ Tbsp poppy seeds

2 – ¼ cups sugar

1-½ Tsp salt

1- ½ cups milk

½ Tsp almond extract

Combine flour, sugar, baking powder and salt in a bowl. In another bowl mix oil, egg, almond extract and poppy seeds.

Add dry ingredients to this bowl and whisk until batter is smooth whisk only to moist. Bake 350 degrees for approx. 30 minutes. Test for done, with toothpick.

Pumpkin Cheese Fiilled Pecan Muffins

2 cups flour

½ cup chopped pecans

1-½ Tsp pumpkin pie spice

2 eggs , beaten

½ cup melted butter

¾ cup sugar

1 Tbsp baking powder

½ Tsp salt

¾ cup pumpkin puree

¼ cup sour cream

1 – 3 oz. package cream cheese cut into cubes.

In a large bowl mix flour, sugar, pecans, pumpkin pie spice, baking powder and salt. In a small bowl mix eggs, pumpkin, sour cream and melted butter.

Add to flour mixture, stir only till blended.

Fill greased muffin tins to half full. Place cream cheese cube in the middle of each muffin and then fill to ⅔ full with batter.

Bake approximately 20 minutes in 400 degree oven.

Pumpkin Ginger Muffins

1- ½ cups sifted flour

½ Tsp baking soda

¾ Tsp ground ginger

½ Tsp ground cloves

⅓ cup sugar

1 egg

½ cup buttermilk

1- ¾ Tsp baking powder

½ Tsp salt

½ Tsp ground cinnamon

6 Tbsp softened butter

⅓ cup brown sugar

⅔ cup canned pumpkin

½ cup fine chopped crystallized ginger

In large bowl, sift together flour, baking powder, salt, ground ginger, cinnamon and cloves. Beat together butter, and sugars in a mid sized bowl until fluffy. Beat in egg and pumpkin. Add flour mixture alternately with milk, blend well.

Fold in chopped ginger.

Fill paper lined muffin pans to ¾ full. Bake in preheated 350 degree oven for 25 – 30 minutes.

Raspberry "Love" Muffins

2 cups flour

1 heaping cup full white chocolate chips

¾ cup sugar

1 Tbsp fine grated orange zest

2 cups fresh of frozen raspberries.

2 Tsp baking powder

1 cup softened butter

1 Tsp vanilla extract

½ cup milk

Sift flour with baking powder, mix in white chocolate chips, set aside.

With electric mixer, beat softened butter with sugar until light and fluffy, add vanilla and orange zest. Mix in dry ingredients in two additions, alternating with milk. Fold in raspberries do not over mix.

Spoon batter into paper lined muffin tins. Bake at 375 degress for 25- 20 minutes. Cool 10 minutes before removing from tins.

Salt Ash, Ugly Muffins

The less than appetizing name for these delicious muffins is derived from the gray-brown lumpy batter. When baked a wonderous surprise. You won't be able to stop eating them.

1 – 15 ounce box raisin bran cereal	3 cups sugar
5 cups flour	5 Tsp baking soda
4 eggs, beaten	1 cup grape seed oil
1 cup raisins and some nuts if you like.	2 cups buttermilk

Combine all ingredients. Cover with plastic wrap so there are no air pockets, and refrigerate. This great make ahead muffin batter will keep well for up to a month.

Bake at 375 degrees for 15 – 20 minutes. Batter makes better muffins when it has rested for several hours, covered and cool.

Savoy Sweet Muffins

2 cups favorite bran cereal

5 cups flour

2 Tsp salt

1 cup Grape seed oil

2 Tsp vanilla

1 Tsp ground cloves

3 cups sugar

5 Tsp baking soda

4 eggs

2 cups buttermilk

1 Tsp ground cinnamon

1 Tsp ground nutmeng

Preheat oven to 400 degrees. Mix dry ingredients in a large bowl. Stir remaining ingredients Mix well. Fill prepared muffin tins ⅔ full.

Bake 15 minutes. Batter will keep up to 4 weeks covered airtight in the refrigerator.

Six Week Bran Muffins

3 cups Bran buds cereal	3 cups all Bran cereal
2 cups boiling water	1 cup margarine
1 ½ cups sugar	1 – ½ cups brown sugar (packed)
4 eggs	4 cups buttermilk
¼ cup molasses	5 cups flour
2 Tbsp baking soda	1 Tbsp baking powder
1 Tsp salt	

Combine cereals and boiling water in large owl. Let stand. In another bowl cream together margarine, and sugars. Add eggs one at a time, beating after each addition. Mix in buttermilk, and molasses. Stir in cereal mixture.

Combine flour, baking soda, and baking powder in an other bowl. Mix thoroughly. Add to creamed ingredients. Stir just to combine. May be stored in refrigerator in tightly covered container fo up to 6 weeks. Fill lined muffin tins as required to ⅔ full. Bake at 400 degrees for 20 minutes.

Variations:

At baking time you can add fresh raspberries, or blueberries or fill muffin cups ½ full add 1 Tsp on cream cheese top with more batter; Bake. You can top with raw sugar before baking to give the muffins a crunchy top.

Smoked Salmon Surprise Muffins

2 cups flour	2- ½ Tsp baking powder
½ Tsp salt	2 Tsp dried dill weed or 2 Tbsp minced fresh dill
I egg beaten	⅓ cup melted butter
I cup mayonnaise	I cup finely chopped smoked salmon
¾ cup milk	12 cubes chevre (goat cheese)

Preheat oven to 400 degrees. Spray muffin tins with non stick oil or line with paper baking cups.

Stir flour, baking powder, and salt in a large bowl. Stir dill into mixture, make wa well in the centre. Combine egg, melted butter mayo and milk, stir in chopped salmon. Pour egg/salmon mixture into the well in the dry ingredients, and blend well with as few strokes as possible.

Fill muffins pans ¾ full. Bake approx 25 minutes untila skewer inserted in center of muffin comes out clean. Cut I inch diameter from top of muffin, insert cheese cube in each. Replace lids and allow chesse to soften. Remove muffins from pans, serve warm.

This recipe will make 6 giant muffins- 3 inch diameter I- ½ inch deep.

Strawberry Macadamia Nut Muffins

¾ cup milk   ⅓ cup margarine or butter, melted

I egg   2 cups flour

⅔ cup sugar   2 Tsp baking powder

½ Tsp salt

I cup chopped fresh strawberries and macadamia nuts.

Divide batter evenly amongst muffin tins that are lined with baking papers, to ⅔ full.

Sprinkle with sugar if desired.

Preheat oven to 400 degrees. Line muffin tin with baking papers.

Beat milk, margarine or butter in a large bowl

Stir in flour, sugar, baking powder and salt just until moistened.

Fold in strawberries and macadamia nuts. Divide batter evenly amongst cups to ⅔ full . Sprinkle with sugar if desired.

Bake 20 – 22 minutes or until golden brown. Immediately remove from pan.

Sunday Morning Muffins

½ cup margarine (soft)   2 cups flour

1 – ¼ cups sugar   2 eggs

½ cup milk   2 Tsp baking powder

½ Tsp salt   2 – ½ cups blueberries (fresh or frozen)

1 Tsp vanilla.

Cream margarine and sugar until fluffy. Add eggs one at a time, then vanilla; mix until blended. Sift dry ingredients and add alternately with milk. Add blueberries and stir by hand. Line muffin pans with baking papers. Fill with batter to ⅔ full. Bake at 375 degrees for 25 – 30 minutes.

Sunken Treasure Pumpkin Muffins

2 cups sugar

3 eggs

½ cup water

1 – ½ Tsp baking powder

½ Tsp baking powder

1 Tsp salt

¾ Tsp cinnamon

½ cup canola oil

1-½ cups canned pumpkin

3 cups whole wheat flour

1 Tsp salt

1 Tsp baking soda

½ Tsp ground cloves

1 Tsp ground nutmeg

2 – 8 ounce packages cream cheese cut into 12 cubes

Preheat oven to 400 degrees, in a large bowl mix together sugar, oil, eggs, pumpkin and water. In a small bowl mix together flour, baking soda, baking powder salt and spices. Ad to first mixture and blend.

Fill baking paper lined muffin pans to ⅔ full. Press a cube of cheese into each muffin. Bake 15 minutes or until tops spring back if lightly touched.

Serve warm. Can be frozen and reheated.

Printed in the United States
By Bookmasters